Hoofprints

Hoofprints

Horse Poems

JESSIE HAAS

GREENWILLOW BOOKS
An Imprint of HarperCollins*Publishers*

Book design by Chad W. Beckerman
The text type is Fournier.

Library of Congress Cataloging-in-Publication Data

Haas, Jessie.
Hoofprints : horse poems / by Jessie Haas.
  p. cm.
"Greenwillow Books."
Summary: A collection of more than one hundred poems
celebrating horses, from ancient times to the present.
ISBN 0-06-053406-0 (trade)
ISBN 0-06-053407-9 (lib. bdg.)
1. Horses—Juvenile poetry. 2. Children's poetry,
American. [1. Horses—Poetry. 2. American poetry.]
I. Title.
PS3558.A176H66 2004 811'.54—dc21 2003049066

10 9 8 7 6 5 4 3 2 1   First Edition

 GREENWILLOW BOOKS

Image on the back of the jacket: Winged horses, Etruscan,
4th-3rd BCE from Museo Etrusco, Tarquinia, Italy;
copyright © Nimatallah/Art Resource, NY.

Image on page vi: A whinnying horse head, bone figure from Mas
d'Aril, Ariege, France; Magdelenian, early Middle Stone Age
(Mesolithic) from Musee des Antiquites Nationales, Saint-Germain-en-
Laye, France; copyright © Erich Lessing/Art Resource, NY.

For Linda Felch

A WHINNYING HORSE HEAD, BONE FIGURE FROM
EARLY MIDDLE STONE AGE

Inspiration for the poem "Rope Halter" on page 29

History

Horse story

My story

Your story

Contents

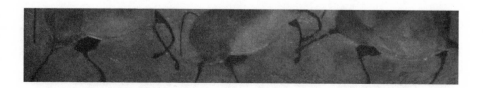

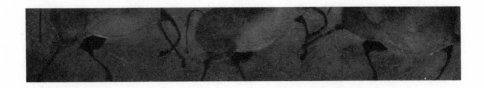

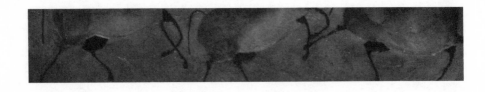

Introduction

I love reading about alternative medicine, for horses as well as for people, and in *Healing Your Horse* I learned something fascinating about acupuncture.

Chi, the essential force acupuncturists work with, runs through the body in pathways called meridians, which are similar in all mammals. But an acupuncturist working on horses can't use meridians below the knee and hock. Sixty million years ago the horse had toes. Now it has a single hoof. The toes remain, tiny irrelevant bones concealed in the long slim column of the leg. The meridians have been concealed as well, squeezed and distorted. Close to the ground, the acupuncture points on a modern horse seem random.

Like those toes, like *chi* itself, hidden truths underlie the horse stories I grew up on—the ones that were supposed to be true.

One of my favorite books is Marguerite Henry's *King of the Wind*, in which the Godolphin Arabian, a foundation sire of the Thoroughbred, is rescued from pulling a cart through Paris streets.

The horse existed. He did, as in Marguerite Henry's book, come to England, via France, from an Islamic royal court in the 1720s. He did father outstanding speed in the Thoroughbred, his descendants are winners to this day, and he did love a cat named Grimalkin.

But he was not an Arabian. He was from a special strain of Turkish horse bred as expensive, prestigious gifts for foreign dignitaries. Calling him an Arabian enabled his English owner to charge a larger stud fee.

As a diplomatic gift horse, the Godolphin Arabian was acquired by a French duke and sold for a high price to a rich

English breeder. He was five years old then and had always been highly valued.

He never did pull that cart.

But if you love that story, here's a true version. In 1965 Louise Firouz, an American woman searching for ponies for her riding school, discovered three tiny, beautiful horses pulling carts through the streets of Amol, an Iranian city on the Caspian Sea. Slender, well-proportioned, and averaging about forty inches at the shoulder—just a little taller than a yardstick—they resembled horses depicted on the seal of Persian king Darius around 500 B.C. The king and the lion he hunts both tower over the chariot horses; before Firouz's discovery this was assumed to be artistic license, or artistic symbolism. Now it seems that the picture may be quite literal.

The horse Louise Firouz rediscovered, the Caspian, has been rescued from near extinction, the Iranian Revolution, and the Iran–Iraq war, and now wins friends around the world for its speed, gentleness, and talent as a driving horse.

Knowing this, I don't miss the Godolphin Arabian pulling that cart in Paris. *King of the Wind* is still perfectly written. The

3

pictures by Wesley Dennis are still beautiful. It's what people used to believe. Now we think something else and tomorrow, analyzing mitochondrial DNA, perhaps we'll know still another version. It, too, will be a marvelous story.

If the stories keep changing, does it matter which one we tell?

I think it does. Horse stories are people stories, our stories. They tell us who we are, where we've been, what we've done. Horses and power go together; telling the story wrong can take power away.

Another tale I've always loved is about my favorite horse breed. The Morgan is Vermont's horse, a unique breed descended from a small stallion of unknown ancestry, Justin Morgan.

Again, not exactly. The Morgan is a close duplicate of the Canadian breed, established in Acadia in 1665. Canadian horses flooded New England after the American Revolution; descriptions of Justin Morgan match descriptions of a good Canadian in nearly every detail.

It's true that the sire and dam of Justin Morgan are unknown. The most popular story, and the one I grew up on, involves a Thoroughbred stallion stolen from a British officer and bred to an Arabian mare. If true, this would be the only time in history that such a cross produced a Morgan, not an Anglo-Arab.

Why the story? I think I know. Vermont was the first state to outlaw slavery, but we didn't outlaw prejudice. Vermonters of British ancestry—for a long time the majority—looked down on French-Canadian Vermonters. Some still do. The quintessential Vermont horse therefore could not be French Canadian. Through many re-tellings, the obvious Canadian ancestry of the horse vanished. The Canadian breed itself declined, as the horses were exported and absorbed into other breeds. Until recently, few American horsemen knew the Canadian breed existed.

Thus, French-Canadian horses and their owners were erased from the story. Just so, the accomplishments of America's Founding Fathers are boasted of, the accomplishments of the Founding Mothers are minimized, and the Founding Slaves who did the heavy lifting are not even mentioned as creators of American greatness.

Now when I look at my Morgan horse, River Echo

Atherton, I see his handsome father, Portledge Steven, fastest Morgan trotter of the twentieth century. I see Justin Morgan, and I see north of him, to stout Canadian horses with docked tails, tormented by flies in summer, worked hard and left sweating in cold winter snows. Thanks to Bonnie Hendricks's *International Encyclopedia of Horse Breeds*, I see across the ocean to Normandy and Brittany, where those Canadian horses originated, where war mingled native draft horses with Spanish Andalusians and Dutch Friesians.

And beyond that, thanks to Deb Bennett's *Conquerors*, I see the horses who became Spanish and Dutch—bred by the Hittites, dispersed when that long-ago empire fell. Farther back there's a profile painted on a cave ceiling. Like a clear-plastic model with bones and organs showing, my horse becomes transparent. Through him I see the slow swing of constellations, the quick eye-blink of human history.

I have always written about horses. I've been asked why many times, and I've never known how to answer. "I love them?" It only invites another question.

Horses are in my blood. I'm an American of German/British

descent; one of the Celtoi, a people knocked loose from central Europe by Asian horse tribes. Like all who survived this experience, we rapidly became horse tribes ourselves.

This heritage is widely shared. Most people of Eurasian, North African, or American descent live where they live, in comparative wealth or comparative poverty, because of conquering horsemen long ago. We have all been changed by the horse, for better and worse. That's reason enough for a twenty-first-century writer to be fascinated by horses.

But *why* do I write about horses? Here's another story. It's a Greek myth, and explains nothing. It only tells us that atop Mount Helicon is a spring guarded by the Muses. It's called Hippocrene, the Horse Fountain; it was formed by the hoof of the winged horse, Pegasus, as he thrust off into the sky. From that day to this, it has bubbled forth the clear waters of poetic inspiration.

And now you know as much as I do.

Ride Back with Me

Saddle up,
  ride back with me.
  You take the Thoroughbred you have lessons on;
I'll ride my fat Morgan.
We'll travel past buckboard wagons, buffalo hunts,
  conquistadores, cavaliers,
  and every sort of infidel invader.
We'll skirt the edge of battlefields,
  follow the tinkling bells of pack trains.
Cling as your mount changes beneath you—
    hack, charger, destrier, rouncy, pad.
The stirrups will drop away,
  the girths will snap—
hold fast.
  At last we'll ride dun ponies,
  bareback
along the rims of glaciers.
While they are horses we will ride them.

Then we'll get off and walk,

 45 million years or so,

our brown-spotted companions

pattering beside us,

  on an ever-increasing number

   of toes.

How the World Makes Horses

She drives the continents apart.

She heats and wets and dries and cools the land,

Makes winter, summer, rainfall, grass.

Then out of a nub of guinea pig–like flesh

She spins her long fantastic thread,

Pulling and twisting and whirling.

She sets up land-bridges,

Spills her animals across,

Walls them behind ice,

Islands them, and isthmuses, and peninsulas them,

And reconnects when they are stubby ponies

Or tall dry desert runners;

Combines the separate kinds she has created,

Throws away ninety-five percent,

Preserves the remnant on a whim,

And twines them at last with the human-thread

She has been simultaneously spinning

To create a two-ply

Of considerable strength.

The Grandmother

I

There were dinosaurs still.
Whales ran over the earth like foxes,
and everywhere strange blunt creatures—
  wolves with squared-off jaws,
    enormous rodents,
      sharp-toothed sheep—
ran and ate and roared and grunted.
No word had yet been spoken,
  and if some thinker had a thought
we have not learned to recognize it.
In the bushes hid
a little brown animal,
knee-high;
Grandmother,
Great-grandmother,
Great-great-great—
call her the Grandmother.
Grandmother of horses.

II

Warm world.
Wet world.
Jungle-covered world.
The Grandmother hid among jungle leaves,
  and ate them.
She padded softly on soft ground.
Mud squeezed between her toes.
She couldn't see far—
        just far enough.
Couldn't run fast—
            just fast enough.

III

The world changes slowly, but it always changes.

A cool wind blowing, not as much rain.

Tomorrow it's colder, only a sprinkle.

Trees dying,

Grass growing.

Nowhere to hide.

Better run.

65 MILLION YEARS AGO TO 1.5 MILLION YEARS AGO,
NORTH AMERICA

I Just Wonder

Were they pretty?
Did they shine?
Were they plump,
Or sleek and fine?

Were they striped
Or were they spotted?
Dappled, streaked,
Or polka-dotted?

Did they smell nice?
And what sound
Did their paws make
On the ground?

Did they squabble?
In a fight
Did they kick,
Or scratch and bite?

Did they squeal
Like colts and fillies?
Were they playful?
Were they silly?

They lived very
long ago.
Still, I hope
Someday we'll know.

*60 MILLION YEARS AGO TO 1 MILLION YEARS AGO,
NORTH AMERICA, EUROPE, AND ASIA*

Evolution

This video moves so slowly
  that motion is impossible
  to detect.
The growth of a sequoia is rapid
  by comparison.
Speed the tape up to make sense of it.
  A short-faced berry eater
    runs out of berries,
      switches to leaves.
  The trees thin.
She drops her head to graze.
Grass screens her eyes.
Is something sneaking?
Her face lengthens.
  Her eyes widen,
    as if in a cartoon,
and migrate to the sides.
  Large and dark, perpetually shocked,
  they brim above the grass-tops.

The foot beside her quickly cropping muzzle
　is not the same foot she began with.
The paw that tracked soft forest floors
　has only three toes now;
the middle one bears the weight.
When she thinks she hears a sound
　that hard hoof spurns hard earth,
and she's halfway across the prairie
　with her herd.

Now adjust the audio frequency.
There is a sound,
　　also undetectable.
It booms and grumbles through the ground
　like the voices of elephants, miles apart.
We do not hear it with our ears.
Our bare feet barely catch
　a small vibration.
Do not expect to understand.

The word is long and spoken slow
and we are only partway through
one syllable.

60 MILLION YEARS AGO TO TODAY,
NORTH AMERICA

It's Alimentary:
PowerPoint Presentation by Miohippus,
late Oligocene Epoch

There are only so many things to eat in the world,
    and several competitors for each.
        As we start to feel the pinch,
    I'd like to propose a bold strategy.
If you'd dim the lights, please?

It's all about cellulose—
    which, I don't need to remind you,
        is the main ingredient of leaves and grass.
The bad news?
        We can't digest it without fermentation.
The good news?
        Neither can the competition.
But reports indicate they're using a new strategy:
    regurgitation.
        Yes.
Believe it or not, they chew, swallow,

ferment their food for a couple of hours
    in a couple of stomachs—they have *four!*—
then burp it up and chew again.
Labor-intensive,
    but it makes pretty efficient use of feedstock.

The direction I suggest *we* take is this:
    ferment our feedstock in a single chamber.
  Disadvantage?
        Less efficient per unit of feed.
Advantage?
        Speed. Our throughput time
    should be roughly half of theirs.
That means we could eat faster—eat *more!*—
    because there's no downtime, no cud-chewing.
Further advantage?
    We don't compete directly.

Let them exploit the low-fiber market;
     we'll *own* high-fiber.
Interestingly, this gets easier if we grow.
    The bigger we are,
        the less energy we need per cell.

So, in conclusion, friends,
I recommend we aggressively go after:
    Fiber. Speed. Size.
It's niche-craft at its best,
and I think it's going to surprise the heck
    out of the competition.
        What do you say?

30 MILLION YEARS AGO, NORTH AMERICA

Global Warming:
What Survives Is Also Beautiful

When you are thinking of ice melting,
Of seasons heating, of sands spreading,
When your heart despairs at beauty ending,
Hug your pony.

Out of rain forests drying and shrinking,
Over the lost lands rising and drowning,
Past ice reaching and ice withdrawing,
Came your pony.

Formed by changing that looked like ending,
He can't see what the future's bringing,
But around corners he's come galloping.
Hug your pony.

TODAY

Przewalski's Horse

The P is silent.
Also the R and Z.
Say "Shah-val-sky."
Don't read the placard
kindly provided by the zoo
to misinform you.
This is not a primitive horse,
not ancestral
to Blaze, or to Black Beauty.
This horse is new,
and beautifully adapted.
The large nose warms
the crystal air
so it will not shock the lungs.
Big feet easily
traverse the bogs.
Heavy body, short ears,
long shaggy coat

keep the claw of cold

from reaching to the heart.

If you want a name you can pronounce,

remember:

  this is the horse the Ice made,

the last Ice, the Würm Ice.

Call her Glacial Horse.

200,000 B.C. TO THE PRESENT,
NORTH AMERICA AND EURASIA

Endless Grasses

We are galloping this sea of grass,

Sunrise to sunset, sunrise to sunset.

No sound but our breath,

No sound but our galloping.

No sound but the wind, and the tall grass shhhing.

The sky is broad and blue and endless.

Endless are the grasses.

We crossed new land where none had been before,

Land from the sea, land between the seas.

Now on and on the grass stretches.

On stretch the herds.

Mammoth and reindeer, bison and rhino,

And horses.

Our hooves beat the earth-drum.

Our voices speak.

Doe to her fawn.

Cow to her calf.

Mare to her foal.

ONE MILLION YEARS AGO,
NORTH AMERICA TO BERINGIA TO THE EURASIAN STEPPE

Two Legs

But

Who is this

Two legs,

Walking out of Africa?

Sleek like an antelope,

Shaggy like a bear.

Smell like a meat-eater.

Slow. Slow.

He can't

Do much

Harm.

ONE MILLION YEARS AGO TO 20,000 B.C.,
LEVANT, EUROPE, AND ASIA

The Great Hunt

Not a needle,

Not a nail,

Not a net and

Not a pail.

Not a shirt and

Not a rope,

Not an arrow,

Not a hope.

Thus it was in oldest times,

Not in yours and not in mine.

Now we sew our clothes of skin,

Now we flake the spearpoints thin.

Hunt the mammoth, hunt the deer,

Hunt the horse, and eat, and cheer.

Round the fire, tell the story,

Tell the daring, tell the glory.

Paint it deep inside the cave,

You and I and they were brave.

Thank them all for food they gave us,

Fat and meat and hide to save us.

It's a good life here, my daughter,

Camped beside the flowing water.

Hear the beating of the drum.

Hear the vast herds, hear them come.

This is how we'll always live.

Herds will give and give and give.

Mammoth roam and wild horse run,

From moon to moon

And sun to sun.

35,000 B.C. TO 5000 B.C., SOUTHERN EUROPE

Rope Halter

It's a rope halter, isn't it,
on this neighing pony?
He's tethered, isn't he,
And calling to his herd?
You've seen a pony call like that,
Tied, and his stablemate departing.

But it's thirteen thousand years ago
And we say, with all our knowledge,
That no horse was tamed then and so
None was haltered,
And we'll never know.

At a cave's mouth
In a green and sheltered valley,
Did someone have a pack pony?
Milk pony?
Decoy pony,
   tied out to lure the others to the spear?

Or are these rope marks

cut into the antler

by our own imaginations?

Is this lonely neigh,

the openmouthed, left-behind look

the mere slip

of an unskilled craftsman's hand?

11,000 B.C., FRANCE

The Colonists

They'd sent out colonists,
  wave on wave—
    the large, the small,
      the many-toed, the single-toed.
Meanwhile,
  ice from the north devoured the homeland,
divided and whittled the herds.
Yet they lived
  many carefree generations,
each believing the pastures
  had always been this size,
each believing that the world
  ended at the ice-wall.
This proved false.
The people from beyond
had seen horses before
and knew well how to hunt them.
The horses did not know how to be hunted.
In the ice-bound meadows

they had nowhere to run,

  no time to learn.

So in America, where they began,

horses ended—or paused.

A long pause: some eleven thousand years.

But out in the wide world

  horses continued,

and at last returned to the home-place,

to find the folks all gone.

60 MILLION YEARS AGO TO 10,000 B.C., NORTH AMERICA
DECEMBER 1493, DOMINICAN REPUBLIC

First Rider

The first rider
  grew heavy on his
    mother's hip,
tugged at her
  ivory beads and she
   balanced him
    on the pack mare's back,
for a rest.

His father laughed.
  "Look at the little chieftain!"
His big sister said,
  "Me too!"
And the boy himself said,
  "Faster!"

11,000 B.C., EURASIA

She Said

She said: I will tie two long poles to the mare; the ends
　　will drag behind her in the dust.
She said: I will drape a hide across the ends to make a
　　sling or cradle.
She said: The load will ride there,
　　Baby, cookpots, puppies, Grandmother.
She said: Dinner's ready. But give the mare this hearth-cake
　　before you come sit down.

MID-STONE AGE, EURASIA
1600 TO 1800S, NORTH AMERICA

Moss

Reindeer go,
Where mosses grow.
Cross the river
Where they've crossed forever.
We go too.
It's what we do.
Same old track.
There and back.

I've seen the horse
Take a different course.
Eats the grass
Our reindeer pass.
Gallops and prances,
Frisks and dances.
He looks free.
Not like me.

I'm going to catch him.

I'm going to ride.

Leave these deer

I've trudged beside.

I'm going to follow

The waving grasses,

Across the steppe

And through the passes.

I will see

All there is to see.

I'll be free.

I'll be free.

*5000 TO 3000 B.C. (TRANSITION TIME IS UNCERTAIN),
NORTHERN MONGOLIA*

New Words

I dared.

I fell.

I draw my breath in small sips.

You, my father,

bring me water on a leaf.

If my ribs heal I'll try again,

though I ride for an eye-blink

and suffer for two moons.

Why?

It will take a long time to tell you.

I must lie here a season,

dreaming the new words

for the new world I saw.

Words for the rippling without effort

like wind in the grass-tops.

Words for the swift-moving

like a small stick on the river in spring flood,

like the arrow loosed toward the prey.

Words for the hoof-thunder when it bears you up,

and when it recedes in the distance

and your ear is suddenly against the earth.

Words for the horizon leaping closer,

and the new seeing from that height.

Yes, bring the shaman.

The future spoke to me—

we must consult.

5000 TO 3000 B.C., UKRAINE

Loose

How long had we lived there?
Forever, I think.
Just below the lip of the valley,
  we sheltered out of the wind;
ten families and our oxen, gardens,
  sheep, and milk-mares.
To each day its task, to each season its measure.
The eagle hung above in the sky-dome
  and we walked beneath it, and were small.

Then—what's this?
Swift movers—horses. With two heads?
No, men from upriver
  sitting their mares
  as a child sits the back of an ox.
We had known these men of old,
  traded with them.
Now we saw that they could become dangerous,
  if we did not grow dangerous ourselves.

We young people—girls, boys—

We tried it. We could.

"A horse is quick," we told the old ones.

"You have to sit quick."

Not all could change.

They remained at the riverbank.

The thatch grew thin,

Like a pony shedding its coat in spring.

The gardens grew smaller.

We visited in winter,

  brought them meat,

    shared their grain.

They are fewer, the villages.

They will not last.

We're loose now, loose on the world,

  like an eagle trailing its jesses,

    like the wild herds themselves.

Wolf-time is on us, bow-time, and sword-time.

When I was young my legs were straight.

Now they're bent to fit a horse's ribs,

  bent as the hoop of the horizon,

    and all the world is moving.

5000 TO 3000 B.C., RUSSIA

Information Superhighway

It's all over the world already.

Can't put it back in the box.

Speeds up everything.

There's a space behind their front teeth.

With a twist of rawhide,

or a bar of something harder,

you can turn and stop them,

even the strongest.

The human race enters a new age.

We cannot guess at the future.

5000 TO 3000 B.C., NORTH-CENTRAL ASIA

Song to My Horse

That was a steep hill.
That was a broad valley.
That stretch between water holes
Held here and there a thirsty skeleton.
With the spring in your hocks,
The lift of your head,
The swish of your long black tail,
You cancel distances.
You make the way level.
You abolish loneliness.

5000 to 3000 b.c., Russia

Bone Story

Under the long low red-purple sheet of clouds
I am seeing a flat plain spiked with grass stems
I am seeing bones and they tell a story
We are kneeling in the grass to read the bones
We are digging softly with a one-haired paintbrush
And we bring up a tooth with a mark worn into it
The mark is a lens, and we are looking back
Seeing, under the cloudsheet,
    on the half-dark plain
The little men riding and the chariots wheeling
    And soon, perhaps,
On our knees in the dust
We will find a bone we can fashion into an earpiece,
    and then we will hear them shout.

Looking back to 5000 to 3000 b.c., Russian steppe

The Horse Camps Glitter

On the steppe's hot griddle,
  Within the sharp rim of mountains,
The horse camps glitter.
Earth-brown,
    horse-brown,
      dung-brown world,
and the brown riders
  make bright rugs,
      bright felts,
Pound gold into tiny, perfect creatures,
Hang them on their shirts,
  Trickle them down
    the seams of their trousers,
And go glittering,
  Catching sun,
    Like a million cobwebs on a morning meadow.

5000 TO 3000 B.C., ASIAN STEPPE

Who Wears the Pants?

We never had pants, before horses.

Never needed them.

A flowing tunic, a jerkin,

Served our purposes.

From a distance, from the rear,

Both looked alike, man and woman.

Among the tribes whose women ride,

  they still do.

But when we divided our skirts into the two tubes,

  the breeches,

most of us horse-tribes made a further division.

There were things fit for men, things fit for women,

And empty air between.

Now ask yourself,

Whose is the whip-hand?

Who holds the reins?

Who's in the saddle?

Who wears the pants?

4000 B.C., ASIAN STEPPE
500 A.D., TROUSERS WERE INTRODUCED TO THE GREEKS AND
ROMANS BY THE HUNS

The Bow-legged Girl

The bow-legged girl has left her bones behind,
her wrist bones with their bracelets,
her delicate neck tipped to one side
under gold coins.
Melted into her hooped rib bones,
battle-armor,
and her shin bones bend
to the shape of a horse's sides.
Her bones are notched
with old arrow-wounds,
her head is dinted,
but don't pity her youth, her early end.
It is certain that she dealt wounds too.
Buried beside her, her bow, her arrows,
a blade with a worn hilt.
She won many battles; this, her latest,
proving beyond doubt
that the warrior world,
was not a man's world only.

In her day you would not have liked to meet her;

walk into the show-barn down the road

  with her on your mind,

and the hair will rise on the back of your neck.

You'll see her kind lording it

in every aisle.

4000 B.C., NORTH-CENTRAL ASIA

Forever

During the long slow stretches when nothing happened
winter came. Everyone sat tight
in little houses of felt or sticks.
Outside the horses pawed through snow for grass,
miserable, but strong, and every colt-crop stronger.
In spring children twined flowers
into the old mare's mane,
played with foals,
and drank and drank and drank the good white milk.
Everyone stretched in the sun,
everyone traveled toward the next fresh grass,
and no one dreamed
that this was not forever.

3000 B.C. TO THE PRESENT, MONGOLIA

Revolution

Revolve: Orbit a central point. Turn on an axis.

Wheel: Solid disk or rigid circular ring
> connected by spokes to a hub.

Cart: A wheeled vehicle drawn by a horse or other
> animal.

Cartwheel: Revolution.

3500 B.C., MESOPOTAMIA

Horse and Ox

An ox is a trestle.
The legs, like table legs,
hold up the long straight spine.
A horse is *sprung*—
up-curved neck, down-curved back,
up again over the rump.
An ox lumbers.
A horse dances.
An ox bulges his eyes, wishing
for a scratch on the brisket.
A horse nudges, scrubs with his lip.
An ox is slow. A horse is fast.
An ox is cheap. A horse costs
everything a man might ever earn.

Looking, at least, is free.

2000 B.C., MESOPOTAMIA

Eagle Speaks

Millennia
We've hung here in the sky.
Sun on our backs, and the broad plain reflects it;
sun on the belly, sun in the eyes.
Once the game ran,
big, small, supper-sized.
Now it's man, man, man.
He's eaten the bison and mammoth,
driven off the wild ox,
tamed the earth itself.
Each field grows one thing,
this, wheat, that, peas, another, barley,
drawing the mice and little birds,
feeding them fat for us, feeding them fine.
Once he walked to the field alone,
dug with his stick.
One heard the hack hack hack.
Now he comes with oxen, the big slow-movers.
They drag his digging stick.

He and his oxen live close to the field,

pace slowly to it,

and slowly back again.

But new things are moving.

Fast little horses off the high plain,

hitched to chariots.

Spokes twinkle in the sunlight,

harnesses gleam,

weapons are bright in the hands of spearmen,

and out across the plains they go,

here a messenger, there a group of soldiers,

far off a battle, a city changes hands,

and the prisoners depart on foot,

weeping,

ox-pace.

We've prospered from his farming, but in future
it seems that man may better serve the vulture.

2500 B.C., MESOPOTAMIA

The Hoofprint of Pegasus

After those people came from north and west,
  and overran us with their horses,
the gods,
    overnight,
acquired new vehicles.
The sun,
  which had formerly traveled by ox-cart,
  proceeded in a golden chariot
    driven by Apollo.
Poseidon had horses, and Ares,
and even she of earth and birth and harvest,
  lady Demeter,
began to appear with a black mare's head,
  and her priestesses were called foals.
Did the gods collude
  with those who overcame us,
    or combine with them,
      or come with them?
It is long ago.

What is known is that

when the horse people came,

  a winged horse

was born from the blood

  of snake-haired Medusa,

that dark old power.

He galloped to the mountaintop,

and mountaintops were not enough for him;

he sprang to air,

  his hoof marking the earth.

Water gushed, sweet water.

Poets,

forever,

drink

from that high fountain,

and tell tales of

gods and goddesses,

and horses.

2000 B.C., GREECE

(No) Contest

The city would be named for the god or goddess
Who gave to people the greatest gift.
Zeus would judge.

Athena struck the ground with her spear.
An olive tree sprouted from the rock—
Shade, oil, wood.

With his trident Poseidon cleft the earth.
From the dark split leaped a pure white stallion—
Beauty, speed, power.

Swift and powerful Zeus chose well.
An olive tree brings only good. The city
Is named Athens.

Yet given the choice between olive tree
And stallion, which would I choose?
Which would you?

2000 B.C., GREECE

Messenger

The chariot rattled through this morning,

Out of the misty east and toward the sea.

The messenger drove standing,

Frowning at the rutted track.

The little horses pricked their ears

Toward our gardens, our mares in the fields.

He pulled up at the well,

And all our Rebeccas went down to draw him water.

First the horses drank,

While he stood wiping out his helmet.

He had no words to speak to them, a bold smile only;

No time to linger either. He settled the collars,

Climbed back in the basket,

And drove away through the notch between the hills.

We boys ran with him till we had no breath.

What message did he carry, and to whom?

We'll never know.

A war, a kingship, prophecy of doom—

Not for folk like us, a message chariot-born.

The message that we took, we boys,

Gathered under the big tree afterward—

Head east, and join the army,

Learn to drive a chariot.

Kick up the dust,

Don't stand here choking in it.

POST 1400 B.C., LEVANT

Hittite Chariot Horse

The life?
I'll tell you—
You're not such a bad fellow.
Didn't want you near at first.
Been with my partner four summers.
You get used to a fellow—
But you're all right.

So here's how it goes.
There's the hard gallops—those are fun.
Sometimes they swim us three times a day.
The washing you get to like.
Can't say as I care for being buttered all over.
Odd smell—don't know why they do it.
Then there are the days they'll picket us,
No food, no water, and a race at evening.
Can't tell when they're apt to pull that.
Still, all in all a good life.

And sometimes we leave here.
I've been across the mountains,
And in a broad plain.
We all go, and the men march too,
Big dust.
And way off you'll see another dust,
You'll smell other horses,
You'll hear them,
And they hitch us, there's the driver and a bowman,
And we're all together, all together,
The hooves drum, the smell of sweat, hot breath,
They loose us, go as fast as you like,
One great mad race,
And the strangers racing toward us.

    That's the odd thing.
    Usually they're pretty careful of us.
    You'd think they'd realize, think they'd learn.
    But every time, somebody gets hurt,
    Somebody's left behind.

My first partner—one horse in two skins, we were—
Ran onto one of their sticks.
Fell, in harness.
I couldn't move, and he stopped answering me.
Smell of blood—like one of their metals.
They cut the harness and left him there.
Careless.

But all in all?
A good life.
Now I've stopped wanting to kick you
I think we'll get along.

1585 to 1190 b.c., Asia Minor (modern Turkey)

Proof

It has taken people with advanced degrees
  months and years of study,
    many papers,
to discover that our fathers
      could do
      what they *did* do.

Assurbanipal, indeed,
  shot arrows bareback at full gallop.
Tutankhamen's chariot
  worked.
King Darius did
  have tiny horses,
    just like that,
and Emperor Mu's horses
    had horns.

Therefore discount no
    fantastic theory.

The fantastic happens daily, even now,
and daily we record it.
In time our descendants will prove
that it was possible.

1361 TO 1352 B.C., EGYPT (TUTANKHAMEN)
1023 TO 982 B.C., CHINA (MU)
669 TO 626 B.C., ASSYRIA (ASSURBANIPAL)
522 TO 486 B.C., PERSIA (DARIUS)

The Race before Troy

Paris, a prince of Troy, has seduced Helen, wife of Greek king Menelaus. For ten years the Greeks have besieged Troy to get her back. Now a quarrel has broken out among the Greeks. Achilles, their best fighter, refuses to enter battle. The Greeks are losing; Patroclus, Achilles' friend and chariot-driver, borrows the hero's armor and goes onto the field, hoping to frighten the Trojans. He is killed by Hector, the Trojan champion. In a rage Achilles rises and slays Hector, then drags the body behind his chariot. But the gods love Hector; though they have not saved his life, they prevent his body from being damaged. Patroclus is cremated, and the funeral games begin.

Sing! the race before the walls of Troy.
Brave Patroclus is dead, his body burned,
his white bones laid in an urn of gold,
sealed beneath two layers of melted fat.
Soon the bones of Achilles, his good friend,
will be laid on top of him,
and the two be buried in one barrow
beside that overthrown and sorrowing city.

But yet Achilles lives, Troy still stands,

though its brave son Hector, tamer of horses,

lies naked, dead, dishonored in the dirt.

Achilles brings prizes from his ships

for the winners of games to honor Patroclus.

For the chariot race, the prize of honor:

a skillful woman, and a three-legged cauldron

with ears for handles, holding twenty-two measures.

The horses of Achilles do not race.

They weep for Patroclus who drove them.

Their long manes flow across the ground.

The quality of the other teams is known

but the gods may dispose according to their whims.

(It is their disposing, after all,

that brought about this sorrow in the first place.)

Apollo makes Diomed drop his whip.

Athena returns it,

and in revenge, breaks the yoke

of Eumelus, the nearest competitor,

drops him in the dirt. His nose is bloodied.

Diomed will win the woman and the cauldron.

Antilochus chides his aging horses;
"I'll have my father put you to the sword,
if you fail to win me second prize."
Galloping hard, they overtake Menelaus
where the rutted road runs deep and narrow.
Side by side there is not room for both.
"Give way," shouts Menelaus.
Antilochus pretends he does not hear.
Prudent Menelaus checks his horses, lest he crash,
and comes third to the finish,
as close to Antilochus as the chariot
is close to the horses' tail ends at full gallop.

Now they all quarrel; a quarrelsome lot,

or they would not have been here

these ten years already

besieging Troy for Menelaus's wife.

Eumelus limps in bruised and bloody,

dragging his chariot and driving his mares.

"Here comes the best man, last," Achilles says.

"I'll give Eumelus the second prize."

Up speaks Antilochus, claiming it.

And Menelaus, to contest the point:

"The boy defeated me by a clever trick,

not the deserving fleetness of his horses."

Youth apologizes, age backs down,

Achilles awards the prizes,

and the boisterous mourners are all satisfied,

save possibly the woman.

Perhaps she too; but this is not her story.

Thus, then, they raced before doomed Troy,
and thus the tale is told;
three thousand years and still the winner
flies to the finish in a hail of gravel;
his chariot barely marks the dust behind him.
Still the sweat rolls down the horses' chests,
and still they gather glory for their masters.

1300 B.C., TURKEY

The Knife Cuts Both Ways

David, extending his kingdom,
  smote Hadadezer by the Euphrates,
    hamstrung his chariot horses.

The neighs of the cripples
    rang down the ages,
to trouble the Christian faith
    of my good friend.

Beware your cruelties,
    you holy warriors;
    the future listens.

1000 B.C., IRAQ

Hakma, Stigrup

The sands of language blow and drift,

building up a small soft dune

around the original word.

Dig deep.

Feel the shape of it.

A stirrup,

from Middle English *stirope*,

from Old English *stigrap*,

from Old German *steigh* (step)

  and *raipaz* (rope)

and there you have it;

stirrup, stair-rope.

Set your foot in it.

Climb on.

Take up the reins of the hackamore,

bitless bridle of the American West;

from Spanish *jaquima*,

from older Spanish *xaquima*,

from Arabic *shakimah*,

from Persian *hakma*.

The wind still blows,

the sands drift and pile the sounds,

or now and then, given time enough,

unpile them,

till underneath the older word

is once again exposed.

Hackamore.

Hakma.

520s b.c., Persia (hakma invented)
300s b.c., China (stirrup invented)
560s, Europe (stirrup introduced to Europe)

Afraid of His Shadow:
King Philip First Sees Alexander's Greatness

He's black,

With a white star,

A blue eye.

He's big, he's fine,

And I, your father, paid dearly for this horse,

Which cannot be mounted.

You think you can?

You see fear in him who frightens others.

You see him start from his shadow,

From all shadows.

You turn his face to the sun.

He is dazzled, he sees no shadows,

And you leap on,

You pat him gently,

You gallop to the horizon,

and back you come.

My son,

My twelve-year-old son,

My son, you are remarkable.

My son, you are no shadow,

And you cannot change this fear in me

By turning my face toward the light.

There is room in Macedonia for one king only,

And I am he, my son.

I am he.

343 B.C., GREECE

Winged Team

Simply a good little chariot team,
Broad-chested, high-crested.
The ears prick, the nostrils flare,
The short-clipped manes spring back like roosters' combs,
And the wings are lifted.

Twenty-three hundred years ago,
Somebody's pride,
They were driven forth like this before the sculptor
And pranced beneath the hot Etruscan sun.
On a pair like this the wings, you understand,
Are really just a slight exaggeration.

200s B.C., ITALY

A Legend of the Great Wall

We'd been building the Wall
  a hundred years already.
The horsemen we sought to fence out
  swirled below us.
They emptied the land of people,
  drove them off as slaves.
Again the government filled the land,
  again,
    again,
      not waiting for us to finish.

When the white horse appeared,
  wandering ahead of the builders,
    we left him alone,
      white horses being sacred.
Was he sent to guide us?
He must have been magical
  to climb a slope like that.
We tracked him with our Wall.

Whatever path he chose,
   we built there, come hill, come valley,
      and when we lost him in a sandstorm
we built five miles from where we'd seen him last.
Finding he'd gone another way,
   we began again,
     from the place where we had lost him.
He may have come from Heaven, after all,
   and it made as much sense
     as anything.

400 TO 214 B.C., CHINA

Pack Ponies

I like to think of pack ponies,
Yellow, brown, and black ponies,
Padded out with panniers,
Trudging up the track.

Where the way is steep and stony,
Where the earth's spine stands up bony,
They plod with their panniers,
Getting there, getting back,

Following a fearsome mare,
Old and witchy sneersome mare,
Following the tinkle
Of the bell around her neck.

The grain, the oil, the peat, the gold,
The things we bought, the things we sold,
Announced all up the hillside
By the bell around her neck.

I like to think of waiting there,

Listening for bell and mare,

Watching for the ponies

To come trudging up the track.

ANYTIME, ANYWHERE MOUNTAINOUS

Roman Riders,

having no saddle,
  or even a cushion,
  preferred
a plump horse
with gentle gaits,
such animals being easier on
the tushion.

A.D. *170, ITALY*

Earnhardt, Adorandus

Maybe you have
a NASCAR T-shirt,
cap, or bumper sticker.
Maybe dead Dale Earnhardt
looks out from your wall.
You join an old club.
Fifteen hundred years ago
in Roman baths,
the names of great race horses
and their pictures
were picked out in mosaic tile,
somewhat longer lasting than
a T-shirt.
Earnhardt, laminated,
joins the roll of honored dead,
with Aura,
Adorandus,
Crinitus,
and Cupido.

550, ROMAN NORTH AFRICA

Ways of Mounting

Choose a short horse.

Stand him in a ditch.

Keep a slave on hand to help.

Put a hook on your spear shaft. Drive your spear
    into the ground, step on the hook and from there
      to the horse's back. Pull out your spear.

Cause all roads to be furnished with piles of stones,
    at stated intervals, for mounting,
      large fine payable to the central Roman government
      for failure to provide same.

Get on once, and don't get off.

Carry a rope ladder.

Take a flying leap.

At some point inventing the stirrup becomes
the obvious thing to do.

300s B.C., STIRRUP INVENTED IN CHINA
560s, STIRRUP FIRST USED BY ROMANS

Horse, Soldier, Arrow

A Chinese soldier stands
before his horse,
grasping an arrow.
Stone point, in stone hand,
touches the stone chest
of the horse.
Some describe the sculpture this way:
"A soldier withdraws an arrow
from his wounded mount."
Others:
"A soldier performs acupuncture,
stimulating his mount before battle."
The horse stands calmly.
Acupuncture is calming;
battle-wounds, probably not.
Without words,
or arrows of direction,
we must let the horse say
if he is healed of the point,
or by it.

600s, CHINA

Is That So?

I want you to know that history is not what you have been
   told.
You have been asked to pledge allegiance to certain facts,
And that is a misuse of schooling, to teach you only
   phrases,
A lulling rhythm to rock your mind to sleep.
I want you to be suspicious of everything—
   and at the same time cheerful, is that possible?
I want you to look them in the eye and ask, Is that so?
And smile, and be quiet, and wait. If you do this
Alternative explanations may emerge.
I want you to practice this in everything—
Paper airplanes, what you wear, anything a politician or
   a lover tells you—
And most of all history, because when someone is telling you
How you got here, and why, and sometimes when,
Something is at stake, for you hearing, for them telling.
So we practice, reading horse books.
"The Arabian horse is the oldest and purest breed."

What do you say?

"*Is that so?*"

No, it isn't so, I tell you. The Arabian derives from older
  breeds,

  Turkmen, Caspian, and others.

It's not even from Arabia, and the Turkmen breeders

Do not consider it pure.

  And *you* say?

"*Is that so?*"

Blessings

Mohammed,
who married well,
said, The greatest of all blessings
is an intelligent woman,
or a prolific mare.

560 TO 632, SAUDI ARABIA (MOHAMMED)

Solomon's Horses in Mohammed's Army

Horses were rare in Arabia.

Really, the place is ill-suited for horses.

Mohammed rode to Medina on a camel—

later, he favored mules.

But horses were his love.

Rumor reached him—

   the remnant of Solomon's herds

ran free out in the desert.

Mohammed traveled there,

   returning with five mares,

wind-swift, doe-gentle.

Riding their descendants—

and several thousand others

   obtained

the old-fashioned way,

by war—

Moslems captured

Jerusalem.

600s, SAUDI ARABIA, ISRAEL

North Sea Farmers

GRANDDAD
DENMARK A.D. 850

The ship is ready, loaded down.
The sea is high, the wind is high,
but I buck the earth-furrow,
plow my ground, sow my seed,
food to harvest in the fall
when we're done a-viking.
Plunder's grand, but can you eat it?
The tide calls, the wind calls.
Viking or farming, time rules,
and we plow with horse, not ox.
They eat more, they cost more,
but horses work the fastest.
Waves are crashing in my ears.
Walk on, boy. Walk on.

GRANDSON

ENGLAND A.D. 925

I don't know why it is.

In spring I've got to hurry.

Itches deep down in my bones.

Plow with oxen? It would kill me.

Can't rest. Can't slow . . .

(I know why. I do.

Don't talk about it.

Not around the family hearth.

It goes back to Granddad:

plowed before he came a-raiding.

Goes back to Grandma:

she rushed to plow and seed a crop.

Come fall they'd creep out,

those still left alive,

and harvest.

One year she came out too early.

Next year the old man stayed.

Now all along these coastal lands
you'll see us plowing fast with horses,
looking over our shoulders at the sea.)

The Fearful Knight

Vast and dark the forests,
lonely the road.
Solitary on his stout horse
the knight approaches,
slow as a crawling ant.
His dull mail gleams
like the shell of a lobster
still dripping from the sea.
Within,
the fearful white flesh
shrinks and shivers.
The round eyes dart
behind the visor.
Do spirits lurk
in those tree trunks?
Rise with that mist?

He startles

at imagined sounds.

Real sounds he does not hear.

His horse is hung with rattles,

clinkers, bells,

to frighten and drive off the spirits.

They alert us,

band of mortal robbers,

that our prey

approaches.

1000, NORTHERN EUROPE

Muzzled

The warhorse is kept muzzled.
His teeth tear the foe in battle,
At other times, anyone else.

The horse is muzzled.
Now who will muzzle the Master?

1100, EUROPE

Riding with the Horde

I think we are half horse,
As the Walkers say.
All day long: rumble of hooves,
Good earth smell of sweat and dust and grass.
Look back on ears and heads,
On manes and switching tails,
Following like a river in brown flood.
Ahead it's just the same,
A long brown river of horses.
Here and there a rider sits his queen mare,
His mare with sour ears, his mare that bites.
Or he is leading her
In obedience to the *yassa*.
No more than once in four days,
May each horse be ridden.
The kindness of Ghengis,
Punishable by death.
There are horses enough to eat one when we must,
To milk, or on hard marches bleed

And cook the blood and eat it as a pudding.

We conquer for the riches, and for pasture.

Pasture for the horses.

Horses for the conquest.

Conquest for the pastures,

For the horses,

For the conquest.

1162 TO 1227, CENTRAL ASIA (GENGHIS KHAN)

Out of the East

If you had a seat slung high,

A hammock in the horn of the moon,

You'd have watched them.

Out of the east they came boiling,

Again,

Again,

Again.

From your comfortable distance,

You might have seen the farmer in the field,

Wife at the hearth,

Child playing on the doorstep.

Nothing moving faster than the slow ox,

Till suddenly the little birds flew up,

A flock of them,

A rabbit ran before,

The farmer looked up.

Wildfire?

You'd have seen before he did the gallopers,

Bows strung.

You'd have seen the big dust, and the

Black smudges of smoke behind,

And you'd have heard it,

  like thunder in the ground,

The hooves, the hooves,

Coming faster than anything comes

  save storm, flood, or fire.

Far up on your moon-seat you'd have seen

Flash of metal, bright blood,

Goods of the house turned out in an instant,

Goose snatched up, lamb across a saddle.

If you'd been up high.

If.

1100s to 1300s, Asia,
North Africa, eastern Europe

A Claim Not Made by UPS or FedEx

That's the messenger—hear his horn?
He gallops to the post house,
  never slacking.
Another man rides out. He leads
  a saddled horse,
and they gallop together, three abreast,
  the riderless horse between—
Ah! He makes the change,
  mid-air, saddle to saddle.
The fresh horse pulls ahead,
  the spent one slows, wringing its tail, and see?
Those puffs of dust down the road? He is
that far already. He has galloped
  a hundred miles today. He'll go
a hundred more, perhaps, before his
    feet touch earth.
By wrapping bandages tight around his body
  he holds himself together,
    though when he dismounts, the bones of his skull

gallop on for hours.

What does he carry?

We don't ask, not even of ourselves,

   and we are not a timid people,

      nor incurious.

With reason it is said,

   well said,

"A virgin with a pot of gold

can cross the empire unharmed,

   carrying the seal of the great Khan."

1200 TO 1949, MONGOLIA

During the Delhi Sultanate

"Why so much about war?"
I'm sorry.
It *was* about war,
and did much to reconcile the populace
to war.
Horses, ever better and more beautiful
to meet the military threat;
gentle, swift, enduring, loyal.
Men arose as well
—yes, sorry,
it is also much about men—
who could bring horses to a pitch of training
we do not attempt.
They could fly a horse
full thirteen feet straight up,
thrust a spear into the howdah
perched atop a raging battle-elephant;
could leap between the sharpened,
swordlike tusks;
the horse would drum the elephant's head
with both front hooves.

Beyond that, you would admit,

nothing shows a man to such advantage

as a prancing, silken steed.

Let the saddlecloths be fringed,

the flywhisks fat,

let the armor's polish flout the noonday sun,

and let the men sit straight but easy,

turning their heads to laugh with one another

as they ride back triumphant to the city:

Will you declare that you are not attracted?

1200s, INDIA

A Lady Laments the Changing Times

Once there was real danger in a joust.
The lances were well sharpened.
Knights killed, dared death,
for a lady's handkerchief
or other favor.
Now there's a wall between the fighters
—can you believe it?—
and the fat louts whack each other
for a purse,
not a lady's love.
Here's what *I* love—
when one of the fools
in all his useless muscle
and his clanking armor
gets hit!
Off he flies
like a milk-pail off a shelf
and clang! he lands,
—unhurt, of course unhurt!—

and the riderless horse,

looking much relieved,

shakes himself

and seeks a bite of grass.

That first unburdened destrier

I name the winner,

awarding it the prize

of my affection.

1400s, EUROPE

The Black Mare's Milk

A pale child,
she does not thrive.
All family cures have failed,
the priest has blessed her,
  and it is left to some
    unusual person—
Let us not be sexist.

    Let us not say,
      always,
      it was a Wise Old Woman.
Often it was a soldier,
  who had traveled far,
    seen many cures;
occasionally a pale scholar,
  well-traveled in lore;
and once in a while
  a person of either sex
    of great age,
who'd been raised on the tale

of his or her own cure;
saying,
    The milk of a mare is sovereign
      in these cases.
Someone who had a mare was importuned,
    the foal tethered as the sky grew light,
      the mare milked at sunrise.
      The pale child tilts the beaker,
and in a few days, Yes! she grows stronger,
    and in a few weeks she is out in the fields herself,
      sister to the foal,
and whatever the reigning religion of that place,
the Goddess who is called Epona
      or Demeter
    or several alternate names
    rejoices
  having brought another back
  from dark to daylight.

5000 B.C. TO THE PRESENT, EURASIA

Something to Remember When Aliens Land

The first American to sit a horse,
   cacique Cãonabo
was nervous, naturally.
"Our King across the sea controls his horse,"
  the Spaniards told him,
"by wearing silver bracelets such as these."
Cãonabo held out his wrists,
   the handcuffs closed,
  and Columbus's laughing soldiers killed his men,
  carried the cacique off to prison.
   He died at sea.
Should they land here
   and offer you a joyride,
I would not buckle the aliens' seat belt
  if I were you.

1494, HISPANIOLA (DOMINICAN REPUBLIC)

Jingle Bells in Tenochtitlan

Listen.

On a quiet night

you may hear the Spanish horses

once again enter the city.

Their riders were not stealthy.

They were too few for stealth.

Boldly they came, with banners

and bright armor,

and all along the horses' breastplates,

    bells.

At every step the stallions

   made merry music.

It echoes yet, on certain nights;

  shing shing shingaling,

    shing . . . shing . . .

      shing.

1519, MEXICO CITY

Bright with Bones

The beach gleams bright with horses' bones.

Discovering this, our man de Soto

recalls that day at the Spanish court

  when he listened to the ravings of de Vaca.

It was known de Vaca's trials had sent him mad.

Eight years lost in Florida,

he staggered into Mexico,

    barefoot,

babbling of the brotherhood of man.

He mentioned also cities,

  gold and emerald cities.

He was a conquistador;

  on the subject of gold

    he should have been reliable.

Now de Soto thinks

  that he did not pay as much attention

    as perhaps he should have

to the rest of the story;

the soothsayer on the beach foretelling death;
the blue bay empty when they returned
from explorations inland,
    ships vanished,
  winter supplies
vanished:
the horses killed in sorrow, one by one,
made into jerky,
    leather sails,
        glue,
and horsehair rigging,
and the desperate voyage on these
    stallions of the wave,
the storm, the wreck, the death of all
save mad de Vaca and black Esteban,
their eight-year,
    barefoot walk among the tribes,
west to Compostela.

At Tampa Bay de Soto

  tips a long, flaking skull with his toe.

White sand sifts through the sockets.

He wonders:

  Where will his own brave bones whiten?

  What part of him, if any, will sail on?

A shudder passes over him.

Perhaps,

even now,

he misses the point

of the story.

1528 to 1539, FLORIDA

Treasure

With colored blankets trailing to the ground,
  armor and harness gleaming,
chain mail polished like woven silver,
  and the tips of their lances touched
    with sunfire,
they followed golden-armored Coronado,
  seeking the seven cities of Cibola.
Finding only sand and corn and Zunis
  they followed the next guide,
    the next tale
of the next incredible city.
Quivira lay always to the north,
  as it does yet; north of nowhere.
In Kansas,
  having found no emerald city,
Coronado beheaded the guide
  and turned back south.
Coronado's horses
  heard the wind in the buffalo grass,
    knew its reminiscent flavor.

They listened
  to the silence of the prairies,
    the waiting emptiness.
They alone of all that company
  perceived the treasure.

1540, MEXICO TO KANSAS

The Spanish Armada Retreats

Horses are swimming in the sea.
Their long manes slide like foam
down the green, glassy wave-troughs.
This way, and this way, and this
the heads point,
seeking land.

But land is far off,
and I am afraid only in legend
do Spanish horses swim ashore in Ireland.

The galleons recede into the distance,
and it is no consolation that,
of those who dumped you overboard
to hasten their retreat,
few will reach home
and none in glory.

1588, OFFSHORE GREAT BRITAIN

On the Death of Major General Humphrey Atherton of the Massachusetts Bay Colony, the Author's First White American Ancestor

Under a Massachusetts moon
  the Major General rides.
His mind is busy with his work:
Keep the Colony
  safe from Indians,
  pure of Quakers,
and extend it toward the frontier,
  the Deerfield Valley.
He does not see the dark wedge,
  black bulk of cow in the roadway.
The horse leaps—
  Over the cow? Away?
History does not reveal this.
Down falls the Major General,
  and does not rise,
  and the Quakers and Indians
    rejoice.

SEPTEMBER 16, 1661, MASSACHUSETTS

Flare-up

Like a prairie fire, the horseback idea
spread across the grasslands.
Get on. Ride. Ride where?
To the neighbor, now so near.
Skirmish, steal his horses,
or slaves to trade for horses;
patrol the land as far as you can ride,
as far as grass extends,
all of life speeding up,
the world instantly smaller.
It has happened before, elsewhere;
the flare-up of war and trade and travel,
the sudden portability of life.
Many times, never exactly like this;
always, exactly like this.
History doesn't repeat itself,
  but it rhymes.

4000 B.C., EURASIAN STEPPE
POST 1680, AMERICAN WEST

Gladdening

Feed them some small treat.
Notice the surprised forward flick of ears,
the lightening and softening
of their large, beautiful eyes.
How kindly they look on you
the next time you approach.
You are not the first to have discovered this.
Soldiers winter-camped
on drear ill-chosen marshes,
where the great cat Starvation
lifted her paw,
allowed men and beasts to creep
a few inches away from death,
and lay wriggling her haunches,
ready to spring—
these soldiers heartened themselves
by saving morsels of biscuit,
warmed themselves, briefly,
in their horses' gladdening eyes.

1700s, EUROPE

Painted Horses

God,
using the brush of DNA
and the palette of all nature,
has repainted them continually;
Stripes, black on white
  on black
    on white,
moderated by subtleties
  of mocha,
    latte,
      ochre;
a sheen of beaten gold
  that He produced from nothing more
    than horsehair.
He loaned us the paint box next.
Generation by generation
  we spattered on spots,
splashed white socks up some legs,
blotted white off others,
  admired and perpetuated
  dapples;

selected snow white,
   milk white,
     cream white
   winter horses,
dun
 roan
    sage-brush gray
   badlands horses,
bay,
    brown,
     black
   night horses,
and pintos
  for bright box canyons,
    where shadow plays with light,
and invisibility is achieved
    by dazzlement.

1700s to 1800s, American West

Unnatural

The horse has four legs,
and fifty-five possible gaits.
European horsemen
   in Baroque riding halls,
   trotting in place between two pillars,
   soaring into the air,
   hopping, kangaroo-like,
   on the hind legs
have declared three gaits
and three gaits only
to be natural;
walk, trot, gallop
(and canter, which is slow gallop).
The rest must be eradicated.
They have been contaminating equine purity
with outlandish movements of outlandish name

rack, paso llano, sobreandando,

single-foot, rahvan, sobre paso,

amble, tølt, paso trocheado,

smooth like an eel, anguilillo,

paso gateado, smooth like a cat,

tranco, tripple, marcha batida,

paso de viaje, placental walk,

since those hipparions left their tracks

drying on Tanzanian lava beds

three and a half million years ago.

3.5 MILLION YEARS AGO, TANZANIA
1700s, EUROPE, THREE GAITS ARE DECLARED NATURAL
TODAY, THE AMERICAS, ICELAND, TURKEY, SOUTHERN AFRICA,
  RUSSIA, MONGOLIA, AND CHINA, AMBLING GAITS ARE STILL
  COMMON

One Master

The horse that won the race

and the boy who rode him

shared one master.

The man said he owned the boy.

Because other men believed

that this was possible

and right

they let him act that way

and told the boy that it was so.

The horse, lacking language,

was never informed.

1600s to 1865, AMERICAN SOUTH

The Gun

I have seen them startle—
    violently—
at the sound of a sneeze.
Leap out of their skin at
    a splash of sunlight on the road.
Yet there they stand
    beside the big gun they drew up,
while it belches and booms and smokes.
The snipers fire, and they
    just twitch.
A bullet doesn't feel like a fly.
This I know.
But they shudder their hides,
    groan quietly,
        drop,
free creatures in the service of the Gun.

How was this accomplished?
I, too, serve the Gun,
    as if this matters,

and destroying other confused men will solve it.

Snipers aim at more than horses, and I

duck my head, as if bullets

felt

like raindrops.

1500s to 1918, Europe, Asia, Africa, America

To Water

Everyone knows—
  You can lead a horse to water,
    but you can't make him drink.
What everyone used to know
  is that when you lead him to water
    he pushes his muzzle in.
He draws deep drafts,
  and with each swallow
    his ears flick back,
      just barely,
like the escapement of a clock.
You can see him swallow from afar,
  or, standing close,
    hear *nk, nk, nk,*

see him raise his head and sigh,
  mumble his lips and the drips fall back,
    stirring the surface of the water.
Then he'll turn, if he likes you,
  push his muzzle to your face.
A wet kiss.

ANYTIME, ANYWHERE

The Groom

Order,
A certain hush,
Light streaming through
High, round windows,
Clean straw,
Oats rustling from the measure,
And quiet clopping on cobbles,
Gleaming leather.
Your wife doesn't own a brush
Like this one you stroke
Down a horse's silken neck.
Your child does not
Feed as well
As him
With his nose in the manger,
And your own body
—which also serves the Duke,
    most faithfully—
Is never tended thus.

The way of the world,

But time will level things.

The Duke's progeny will have horses,

  but no servants.

Yours will have horses,

    but no master,

And it comes out the same—

Order

In the stables,

Disorder

In the houses,

And all about equally

Satisfied.

1700s to present, England

1848

The earthlid shuts out the day,
And deep down, down in the dusty dark,
Ponies walk, pulling the laden coal tubs.
For years, children did it.
In some workings, even they
Couldn't stand upright, had to crawl.
Parliament, after much debate,
Forbade it.
But factories,
Railroads,
Houses,
Need coal to burn,
Whether it's cruel to come by coal or not.
Then we remembered
The waist-high ponies of Shetland.
The hard workers, the heavy haulers.
We brought them down, and down they'll stay,
Underground working, underground stabled.
When they die,
The grave should feel familiar.

1848, ENGLAND

Foxhunt

"The unspeakable in pursuit
  of the inedible;" yet—
the horn's brave, tinny sound
unspooling across the fields,
the bright red coats,
welcome dots of contrast
in all that green,
dogs' tails curved up
in mindless innocence,
and horses, horses, horses.
The rhythm and balance of their slender legs,
their darks and tans and grays,
the nervous heads thrown up,
and all the ears arrowing one way,
back or forward—
and the great runs,
the daring, fence and ditch and hedge—
O, forgetting poor Reynard and his wife,
pursued,
a foxhunt is a lovely thing.

LATE 1800S, ENGLAND
QUOTE FROM OSCAR WILDE, 1854–1900

Road Apples

Think the city's smelly now?
Imagine! It's eighteen eighty-five.
Every cab, every streetcar,
every fire engine, every hearse,
is pulled by horses.
They call them hay burners,
but I hate to say,
they don't *burn* hay, honey,
they process it!
You wear a long light-colored dress
down to the ground,
right down,
with a stiff pleated ruffle
and a petticoat beneath.
Boys are hired
to sweep the crossings,
but it's not they who do it, girl,
it's *you*!

1885, AMERICA AND EUROPE

M.A.D.D. (Modernity Against Drunk Driving)

Drinking and driving
  never mixed
    except
certain old men
  poured into buggies in town
found themselves
    next morning
waking safely
  in their own dooryards
while the horses
    grazed.

1800s to 1940s, North America

Clever Hans

Clever Hans
could do arithmetic,
his owner claimed.
It could not be true;
a horse could not
paw sums out with his hoof,
stopping,
always,
at the right number.
After much study,
scientists pronounced.
All Hans did,
they said,
was notice
the tiny,
unintended
lift
of a questioner's head
when he had pawed

the correct number
of times.
Turning away,
the scientists
failed to notice
a tiny
lift
of Hans's
head.

1900, GERMANY

Foolish Creatures

They're silly creatures, really.
A sound in the brush, a blowing newspaper—
Before you know it they're down the road,
    hellity-larrup—
And your buggy's smashed, and maybe you are too.
It'll be safer when everyone drives a car,
And we don't have to depend on such
Foolish creatures.

1910, NORTH AMERICA

Abandoned, 1919

Your brothers died
at the dry billabong.
You, strong enough to travel
to one that still held water,
lived.
They gathered you and trained you,
put you on ships
(a hundred twenty thousand of you)
and there in the land of pyramids
they rode and rode and rode you,
fought and marched and died on you.
One nine-day trek you watered three times only.
Eight of your brothers died; not you.
They did not shoot you either.
Not the enemy,
not your rider.
When your country would not take you back,
lest you bring disease,
your brothers folded their legs

and dropped in the sand;
one neat shot behind the ear,
friendly fire.
Some hands trembled, some eyes wept,
and your rider wouldn't do it,
but left you to your fate.
Now, war-horse,
you pull a vegetable cart in Cairo,
forage through dispirited lettuces,
chew a watermelon rind,
while at home they build a monument
and mourn their faithlessness.
It is the kind of story they like to turn
over and over in their hands.

And you?
Is Australia's sun less hot
than this Egyptian one?
You thirst, but you have always thirsted.

You are no thinner than the man who drives you.

Are you nostalgic for the nine-day trek?

Do you long for the dry billabong?

What promise was ever made to you,

son of starvation,

that has not been kept?

1914 to 1919, Australia and Egypt

Hands

Where are the hands?
They combed the reins
   between the fingers—
an eight-up is driven
  with hands and voice only.
The hands are too full
   of rein
to hold a whip,
and the reins hurt,
  their edges must be beveled,
  not to cut the hands,
and eight horses
  must pull evenly,
   steadily,
  and where are the hands,
big-knuckled hands
that picked up the reins
  and picked up the teams
  and got the circus

from train depot
  to empty lot?
Where are the hands?
Not the act, not admired,
but they combed through the reins,
  without thinking,
and leather fountained
from between the fingers,
and intelligence spoke
  to intelligence,
each way, along the lines,
    and where . . . where are the hands?

1930s, UNITED STATES

Big Top

Hot wind snaps the milk white canvas.
Scents mingle:
popcorn, cotton candy, elephant dung,
and the musk of tiger, lion, bear.
As regular as a gear the dappled horse
circles in the center ring.
A girl in tights and green sequins
cartwheels on his back.

If thought shone like a beam of light
you would see two cones of it
reaching past each other.
That boy in the front row seat
who knows only small-town America
yearns toward wild animals,
yearns toward danger—
even as much danger
as a cantering Percheron
represents.

And the Percheron,

cantering his perfect circle

flares his nostrils,

samples the hot mingled streams of air,

seeks even as much grass as grows

in a sour vacant lot,

even as much freedom

as a small-town backyard.

The two cones graze in passing,

widening farther and farther

into the unknown.

1930s, UNITED STATES

The Dutch Horse

The farmer holds up
  your black hard hoof,
nail and hammer in his hand.
You are not afraid.
He never hurts you.

But *this* hurts. Hard and straight
  the nail drives into your sole.
He strokes you. His voice is gentle.
"Sorry," he says.

A few hours later he leads you out.
You're limping.
He trots you up and down the cobbles.
The man in uniform, the man with
  the black, twisted cross
    on his cap,
      says,
"Your Dutch horses seem
  terribly prone to lameness
    all at once!"

When he is gone your man
  leads you to the stall,
    sits down *thump*! in the manger,
leans his sweating forehead on your neck
  a little while.

"Now," he says at last,
"let's treat your foot."

1941 TO 1944, NAZI-OCCUPIED HOLLAND

Triumph

The car is
Up to the axles in mud.
It's nineteen forty-eight, most roads are paved,
But this is Vermont in April.
Mandy harnesses the team—
  Chub and Sailor, the good farm horses,
  Always well-behaved.
  A child of eight can hitch them,
  Usually.
They see the car.
They lift themselves, they swell.
Their walk was slow and heavy;
Now they prance, the harness creaks and jingles.
Thus their forefathers entered the lists,
Carrying knights to a joust.
Mandy swings them round.
They're trampling,
  lunging, blowing.
"Whoa, there! Whoa! Now stand!"

It takes the shouts. It takes his farmer's strength.

They're not afraid. It's pride,

Showing off before the beached machine.

"Hup!" They surge and hit the collars.

Leather groans, their hooves dig in.

With a *suck*! and *snap*! the car comes free.

Prrr! *Prrr*! The breath blows through their nostrils,

And Mandy says, No.

No, you can't pay me.

1948, EAST DOVER, VERMONT,
MANDY TREVORROW, MY GRANDFATHER

Company for Breakfast

Ashton Timson lived alone, up there on the hill.

Bred good work stock.

One year a mare died on him.

Ashton raised her colt on a bottle.

It did all right.

Some folks came up to visit one morning.

Near the house they heard talking.

"Ashton must have company!"

They knocked.

He came to the door.

Behind him in the kitchen,

Was that good-sized workhorse colt.

"I was lonely, and so was he," says Ashton,

"So I asked him in to breakfast."

1940s, WILLIAMSVILLE, VERMONT

Means of Transport

I have other ways of getting around the neighborhood.

Easier to get in a car and turn the key,

Or lace my sneakers tight and walk,

Than travel to the farm, catch and groom you,

Cover your shivering hide with fly spray,

Girth on a saddle,

Persuade you to accept the bit,

Put on a helmet,

And travel a few miles

In a circle.

I have no better way to measure myself.

Today, this second, am I alert enough?

Do I have patience?

Can I work without ceasing when it's important?

Will I take an hour persuading you to see it my way

   and walk, not run or jig or sidle

      across this field?

And when it's not important can I see that? Can I laugh?

Give up? Say, "All right, Friend, you win!"
You, my unnecessary creature—
My thousand underutilized pounds of speed and power,
Are my best means of transport here.
Together let's explore the neighborhood.

TODAY

Epona Considers Her Current Position

I was

Our Lady of the Foals,

Great Mare, Great Queen, Great Mother.

Rhiannon and Macha

were some of my names.

Lady of the regiments,

Queen of stable lads and mule drivers—

Horses ate from my lap.

Horsemen rode before me in homage.

I eased childbirth.

Forgotten for some centuries,

I did not cease to be,

and like all patient things,

I rise.

All is not yet well.

I would not suggest it.

No longer are white stallions driven into the sea,

sacrificed to Poseidon.

Hides and skulls no longer sway
on poles, near sacred springs.
The cavalry charge
is almost a thing of the past.
Yet growing colts are raced to ruin,
whipped to excite them
before they enter showrings,
and it's still hard to be
a beast of burden anywhere.

But observe:
the quiet stable,
multiple, costly robes,
deep bedding, mattresses, even,
and boxes of baked treats, bags of carrots,
plastic tubs of neutraceuticals—
  in shark cartilage, in perna mussel shell,
  brother Poseidon begins to repay his debt—
and retirees live long past usefulness,

as once in Ireland,

two thousand years ago

an old mare fed on oatmeal

saw thirty summers.

The stables swing back

toward shrine.

My accolytes study ancient arts.

I am encouraged.

TODAY

Advice to a Young Woman

Beware of Cupid's bow, my dear.
That bow wasn't curved for sweetness.
Curved for power, curved to clear
A horse's neck, make killing easy—

You aren't listening, my dear.

Beware the hobby horse, my dear.
Your girl will gallop, wave her sword,
Act just like a hobelar,
Skirmisher in a savage war—

Are you listening, dear?

Don't give your girl a pony, dear.
A pony's not a lightsome thing.
She'll grow up strong, she won't beware,
She'll make her own decisions—oh!

Dear, you aren't listening.

1000 B.C., CENTRAL ASIA (COMPOUND BOW)
1269, IRELAND (HOBELARS)

Horse Whisperer

We stand in a circle
    around a man,
   around a horse,
Watch the horse watch
    the man

Listen!
   The whisperer!

He is original,
   he says.
Is it possible?
Every one before him
   was a brute?

   The whisperer!
    Listen!
He . . . he says . . . he . . .

Pardon me.
When I see one man instructing
      a large group of women,
   I tend to feel
         sceptical.

      Listen!
He says . . . he says . . .

Is it true? Does he speak true?
      Truth is truth
      but every truth
may be spoken for a reason.

He says . . . the whisperer . . .
      he says . . .

Listen! Does he set you free?
   The truth will set you free.
Tomorrow, could you talk to the horse?
      Alone?

Does he say, Pass it on?
    Does he?

He whispers . . . he whispers . . .

If it's true,
    let him set it free.
  If it's true,
    he doesn't need
      to hold it.

Shhh! The whisperer!
He says . . . he says . . .

    He whispers too loudly.
    I can't hear
    the horse.

TODAY

He Races

He holds himself back.
The others walk across the field
toward the voice calling,
"Horses! Grain!"
He eats a bite of grass,
drops dung,
stands still for half a minute,
head high,
ears back.
Then squeal,
buck,
(fart!)
and fly across the field.
The timing is exact.
Ahead of the others
he sweeps in through the gate.
Those are the facts.
Science does not encourage us
to consider his motivations.

TODAY

155

He Organizes His Herd of Three

The gate is opened.
The lane leads out to grass.
The Belgian, young and pushing,
surges through.
But there is a certain order,
a fitness of things,
to be preserved.
He hurls himself at the Belgian,
a spear,
driving the bigger horse
back through the gate.
Mill and mingle, turn back, turn back,
—minutes of grazing lost—
until he has the ancient mare in front.
He walks at her flank,
a Boy Scout,
escorting her.

Abrupt halt and backward step

at the hungry Belgian.

Just a minute, bud!

The mare,

ears forward, queenly,

leads them out to pasture,

reprising her former role.

TODAY

This Rider

This rider,
in black jacket, white breeches,
is accountable for each step taken.
Each hoof touches earth
precisely to her bidding.
Cadence, elasticity,
metronomic rhythm,
even the ears,
even if the tail swishes,
or does not,
is her responsibility.

This rider slouches.
In each direction
he sees miles and miles
of miles and miles.
Get over the ground,
look at fences,
look at cattle,

then eat, sleep,

do it again tomorrow.

Let the horse shuffle

any old how,

as long as

it doesn't

raise a blister.

This rider goes as fast as fast can go

for less than three minutes.

Ideally, she doesn't get killed.

Ideally, she'll do it again,

three or four times an afternoon,

ending as often as possible

ahead of all the others.

This rider stays on

—that's all—

eight seconds.

Legs fly loose,

spurs scratch fore and aft,

and then at last the whistle blows.

Let go!

This rider

sits

motionless

in a tall

narrow

sentry box

outside

the palace,

pretending

not to hear

what people say.

And this one hopes
the judge did not see that.
If the mistake was overlooked
she'll win.

TODAY, UNITED STATES AND UNITED KINGDOM

West Palm

Under striped tents,
Beside sheets of water, canals
Where crocodiles lurk,
The jumpers, costing
Half a million dollars
Each
Live all winter;
Exercised, groomed, groomed, exercised,
Several times a week
Entering a ring full of skyscraper jumps
To leap them, one by one.
The thin rich riders,
Or the thin poor,
Richly sponsored,
Talk on their cell phones,
Traverse the grounds on
Golf carts,
Trail their little dogs behind them,
Lose a few to crocodiles.

And Mexican grooms earn
Seven hundred a week
Under the table,
Polishing the expensive,
Living sculptures.
By this means, it is believed,
The best rider is discovered,
The best horse brought along.

TODAY, *WEST PALM BEACH, FLORIDA*

Therapeutic

Her legs aren't right.
She's never even walked,
she can't talk all that well,
and this isn't riding, really—
being led in a circle
on a placid nag—
is it?

    Height,
    large warmth,
    scent rising,
    motion carried up
    moving the body
    that has never moved itself,
    and the gracefulness of the animal
    and the animalness of the grace—

she smiles.
The horse and I walk on.

TODAY, UNITED STATES

Mangalarga Marchador

Now there's a horse I'd like to have;
a Mangalarga Marchador.
The name is lots of fun to say,
and that is what I want him for.

His *marcha* is so comfortable,
my Mangalarga Marchador;
he's swift and smooth and bold and kind,
but the name is what I want him for.

1740 TO THE PRESENT, BRAZIL

Innocent Engines of War

Over the ground where chariots once clashed,
  and chariot horses trampled men to rags,
    charioteers' descendants drove
      descendants of chariot horses
        to trip off land mines.
Still,
  a horse will bear a human touch,
  a human will seek out a horse.
Harm on harm throughout the generations,
  but death cuts the thread,
    a fresh knot is tied,
    a foal looks out of new eyes,
and is seen by the new eyes of a child.

1980s, IRAN AND IRAQ

Behind the Supermarket

Hitch rail, horse droppings,
behind the supermarket.
It's Amish country.

TODAY, UNITED STATES

Efficient

Sure, you could grow soybeans,
And press the oil out,
Mix it with lye, and turn it into diesel,
Run your tractor on that.
Or you could ferment manure and make ethanol,
Chip wood and gasify it;
But why deprive yourself?
What's the hurry? Want to get off your tractor,
  Listen to the breeze,
  Go fishing?
I hear the breeze behind the horses.
I fish poems out of the sky
As they tread down the rows,
Weeding my food,
Weeding theirs.
I've got no farm surplus to drive the prices down.
They eat my surplus.
Grow the fuel,
Make the fertilizer,

Spread it,

All with the one unit.

That's what *I* call efficiency.

TODAY, AMERICAN MIDWEST

Peasant Eyes

If you're on horseback somebody resents you.
America's the refuge of the peasants,
and while some ride, other folks remember.
Slaves of horseback people were never allowed to mount.
The emperor on his moving throne disposed of men.
He gave his mounted muscle land and privilege,
seats in the Senate, seats at the Coliseum.
He tried to bind their horseback power to him;
churchmen tried to bind that power to God.
They called it the Order of Equites, in Rome;
in France, chivalry, which is cavalry.
Cossacks, Kazakhs, always came on horseback,
to steal the silver and spoil the featherbeds,
and the general up on horseback gripped his whip,
sending the infantry into No Man's Land.
The foxhunt ran across the poor man's garden
like a dozen hand grenades among the cabbages.
When you mount, most innocent of riders,
seeking mystic oneness with your horse,

it's not just little horseless girls

who look up, squiggle-eyed;

it's all who feel the peasant in their bones,

whether they know that's what they feel, or not.

1000 B.C. TO THE PRESENT

Down the Side Street

For certain people the city breathes
only when clop clop clop
rings down the side street.
Officer on a chestnut horse?
Carriage-load of tourists?
What matters is that suddenly an animal—
the animal, the ultimate—
has made the pavement musical,
enriched the atmosphere.
His mane has floated
in the wind of his own making.
His legs have sectioned off the city
stride by stride.
He has slowed the rush, and hushed the noise,
and the hot air streaming from the grates
with its cooked smell,
is all at once refreshed.

TODAY, UNITED STATES

Dappled Things

I don't want you to be fooled by words—
"wondrous creatures, magnificent beings,
  embodiment of freedom,"
    et cetera.
There are those for whom they are
  meat.
Food on the plate.

They are not untamable.
It is because they are, in fact,
  quite tamable,
that they live in song and story.
Untamable is a rhino—
  unglamorous cousin.

They're not free. Not now. Not hardly.
What's less free than a mare on the urine line
  perpetually peeing into a tube,
giving her hormones for women's menopause,
  her foals for supper in Paris?

They're not always even beautiful.
Wretched little unfed hardworked scrubs,
  no lovelier than sawhorses.

Don't buy those gift-shop words.
Look.
Look at the whole,
  piebald, polka-dotted,
glory-be-to-God-for-dappled
    thing.

TODAY

Race Riders

Mongolian children
in bright garments
gallop toward the finish
of their fifteen-mile race.
The winning rider
is five years old.
Yes.
Five.
What is the meaning
of a five-year-old like this?
At the identical moment
that she learned to walk,
she learned to ride,
which is not mere sitting,
but controlling
a horse ten times her size.
What could a child like this
not do?
What doors could fear close to her?
She bestrides the world.
Its rocking makes her smile.

Simultaneously

on the other side of the globe

a man starved and sweated and puked and purged

to child-size

rides a three-year-old horse

whose bones have not stopped growing

just one mile and a quarter

to cross a finish line

at Churchill Downs.

The man has shrunk,

the girl, enlarged herself.

What are we supposed to make of this?

TODAY, MONGOLIA AND AMERICA

Buzkazhi

The three-mile field
holds a thousand players.
Afghans.
You have seen them on TV:
enemies allies victims killers
players.
In spite of everything
these horses are alive.
In spite of everything
the game is still worth playing:
This tussle
over a stuffed
animal skin
for glory
and some cash—
how alien to Americans.
How unheard-of.

2002, AFGHANISTAN

If Required

The Grandmother's toe bones
Lie up close
Invisible
In the smooth
Piston
Leg
Of her descendants.
Unnecessary,
Now.
But if toes, in future,
Are required,
There they are.

The horses of Iran
Graze wild in the hills.
Unneeded, they were
Set loose.
Nature crafts them,
Hardy,

Frugal,

Smart.

Unnecessary,

Now.

But if horses, in future,

Are required,

There they are.

TODAY

The Mid-Air Moment

I love the sudden silence,

the mid-air moment

when no hoof touches earth,

and if you're watching

you draw your breath in long,

and if you're riding you know

whether you've caught the arc of this leap

or were left behind,

are balanced,

or are not;

and if you're the leaper

you know what flying is

and no one knows

—watcher, rider, leaper—

how the landing will be,

the beginning of the next big stride

or somersault;

and if falling, will you fall free, alone,

or in a tangle;

untouched,

or beaten under landing hooves?

Oh, the mid-air moment is the one

when all is well,

and everything may yet

turn out all right.

TODAY, UNITED KINGDOM AND UNITED STATES

The Color of Heaven

In the emerald pasture
sunlight glistens
along each blade of grass.
You think—
　To them, that looks like heaven.
It does—
　gray heaven,
　　shading from gray violet
　　　to gray mauve.
That scent, the smell of greenness,
　smells gray to them,
and of itself is enough
to make gray beautiful.
They do see blue, scientists tell us.
They see red.
Apples stand out brilliant on gray trees
　as in a colorized photo from long ago.
When they were tiny fruit-eaters,
　　berry-eaters,

this would have been useful.

Still, the joy of green

   being what it is,

you could cry to think they never see it.

When they reach true Heaven

I hope their ethereal eyes

  are given another set of cones

   and suddenly

green breaks out,

color matches scent,

  and they neigh,

Hallelujah!

Afterword

On WAMC, the Albany, New York, public radio station, I once heard Dr. Steven Leibo say, "History doesn't repeat itself, but it rhymes often enough."

I scrambled for pen and paper. I was working on this book, and nothing was clearer than the strong, insistent rhymes in history, prehistory, and evolution.

The world has made horses—or animals that function like horses—twice. In North America, tiny four-toed eohippus became equus, a horse. In South America, separated from the north for millions of years, three-toed diadiaphoros evolved into swift, single-toed thoatherium, a horse in all but genes. When the

Americas rejoined, thoatherium was unable to compete with equus and became extinct.

Horses also spread into Eurasia and North Africa, where they met early humans. We knew what to do with horses: hunt them, eat them. Eurasian equines met us when we were technologically unsophisticated, and were able to coexist with us, growing warier as we became better hunters. Later, in North America, horses that had never seen a human encountered advanced Stone Age hunters. They rapidly became extinct.

In Eurasia too, horses dwindled, and by six thousand years ago they were nearly gone.

Then someone in some small settlement in the Ukraine, a dot on the vast grassland, a speck under the wide sky, discovered how to partner with horses. It changed everything, for horses and for humans.

A dead horse can feed you for a week. A live milk-mare can feed you for years. She can carry burdens on her back, or drag them in a slide-car or travois. You can ride her. You can get places faster than you ever dreamed possible. After a while you start to realize that there's no reason to stay at home, or even have a home. You can travel, raid your neighbors, move on to good grass, forever.

When horse met wheel, somewhere on the fringe between nomadic steppe and settled civilization, another revolution took place. The wheel had been a heavy, crude thing, meant to turn slowly behind oxen. Now it was possible to unite it with a horse's speed. People took a fresh look, used new designs, carefully considered which was the best wood for every part—and the chariot was born. Rapidly following came chariot warfare.

The chariot was a terrifying weapon, faster than any human. Generally one man drove while another wielded a bow or spear, but the horses themselves were also weapons, able to overrun and trample an infantryman. On favorable terrain, if you had chariots and your enemy didn't, you won. Thus, an obscure Asiatic tribe, the Hyksos, overthrew the Egyptian pharaohs.

The pharaohs regrouped, made a comeback, and initiated a regional arms race: bigger chariots, better horses, advanced strategies. Chariot warfare was the rule from Ireland to China for over a thousand years.

Meanwhile on the steppe where horsemanship was invented, the tribes were busy. They'd been riding horses for millennia, but now they came up with an innovation that made mounted warfare practical: the recurved bow. It's the familiar Cupid's bow we see on Valentine's Day cards—short, curvy, powerful. The small size made it possible to shoot in all directions from horseback, as the bow cleared the horse's neck easily.

The tribes descended again on the settled lands, and made chariot warfare obsolete. A ridden horse was more maneuverable than a chariot and pair. Mounted warriors could operate on rough terrain, travel swiftly, and strike at will.

A new era of conquest and empire began. The center of power swayed back and forth across the Eurasian continent, depending on which people made the next innovation in horsemanship and organization. Persians, Macedonians, Romans, Huns, Arabs, Mongols all ruled in turn, aided by the stirrup, heavy armor, light armor, and various cavalry tactics.

The most unstoppable power of all was the one that looked most primitive: the Mongol horde. In reality Genghis Khan had carefully thought out and codified his rules of war and society, the *yassa*. But the Mongol empire rested on the ancient power of the steppes: absolute familiarity and comfort with the horse. A Mongol was said to be able to perform all bodily functions on horseback. Even today, many Mongolians are brought up on horses. The fifteen-mile Tsagaan Sar race is ridden by children as young as five.

Between fending off mounted invaders, European countries developed a horse-based class system. Land was given to warriors in exchange for loyalty. Known as chivalry in western Europe, it solidified a caste system in which those born into the nobility inherited privilege, and everyone else inherited hard work. (In India the caste system that persists to this day is a relic of the light-skinned horsemen who invaded from the north, and proceeded to grade society according to degrees of whiteness.)

In sport, too, horses served the elite. In England horseracing was called "the Sport of Kings"; dukes, earls, and very rich commoners got to play, but racing was at various times forbidden to the lower classes. Therefore the breeders who developed the English Thoroughbred were, for the most part, from the nobility. One prominent exception was Oliver Cromwell, a commoner who for a time was leader of Parliamentary England. He imported the first horse of Oriental blood to play a prominent role in Thoroughbred bloodlines, Place's White

Turk. Though not noble, Cromwell was a military man of great power.

Away from the centers of civilization, horses remained in more general use. On the steppe the tribes used them as they always had, for food, milk, sport, and transport. After Spanish conquistadores returned them to America in the 1500s, horses were used by many native tribes of North and South America in hunting and warfare. Among the British and French colonies the hold of class systems relaxed, and common people had the choice to race horses, if their religion tolerated it.

Wheeled vehicles only gradually came into general use. Wagons need roads, and road building implies an organized government. The Roman roads were the first in Europe, but they lapsed into disrepair with the fall of the Empire, and wheeled transport waned for hundreds of years. Only in the 1600s, as the feudal system of chivalry began to fade—done in by the long bow and gunpowder—did a surplus of horses become available for wheeled transport.

Other working horses came into common use in the 1700s as the Industrial Revolution began. Ironically, the movement that would eventually replace the horse was heavily dependent on horses for more than two hundred years.

The Industrial Revolution needed horses not only for transportation and power; it made their use in agriculture more practical, as larger and more efficient farm implements were invented and brought into mass production. In North America vast tracts of prairie land—the original home of the horse—were cultivated using giant teams; thirty were often hitched to one combine. American horse-drawn agriculture was a cutting-edge operation.

Then, abruptly, it was rendered obsolete by the tractor. Thousands of horses were slaughtered. Many breeds of draft horse nearly disappeared.

But everything comes around again. Today there are societies dedicated to the preservation of old breeds of livestock. There is a Slow Food movement to counteract the mass-market fast-food culture. Thousands of American farmers use horses, which are gentler on the land, non-polluting, and self-reproducing. A small-implements industry has risen up to serve the twenty-first-century horse farmer, and innovations continue.

Horses are still the best way to handle cattle, and the best horses for the job are usually of Spanish derivation. Bullfighting, the ancient, fatal dance between horse and bull, bred cow-sense into the Spanish horse that still expresses itself in American mustangs and quarter horses.

On the Asian steppe horse milk has never gone out of fashion, and many Russian breeds have been developed for their milking ability. Now horse milk is being rediscovered in Europe for its unique health-giving qualities.

The urine of pregnant mares is also harvested for the manufacture of hormone replacement drugs. In many European countries horse meat is regularly eaten, and the old European draft breeds are raised more for meat than for work.

From its low tide six thousand years ago, the horse has become one of the most successful of domestic species, with sixty million horses living all over the world. It has returned to its ancestral home in North America. In Mongolia, Przewalski horses again live wild, protected by the species that once hunted them to near extinction.

And on a ranch in Idaho lives a strain of horned horse, the Moyle. They descend from horses of legendary toughness once owned by the Mormons. Long, loose, and flexible, almost snakelike, with spleens and livers twice the normal size, Moyle horses make extraordinary endurance mounts, frequently winning the one day, one-hundred-mile Tevis Cup Race.

They hark back by some undiscovered byway of history three thousand years, to the Dragon Horses of Zhou Dynasty China (long considered mythological), which also had horns and could run two hundred and fifty miles in a day.

It rhymes.

Glossary

ALEXANDER THE GREAT—became King of Macedonia in 336

B.C., when his father, King Philip, was assassinated. He had conquered

an empire reaching from Greece to India by his death in 323 B.C.

APOLLO—Greek god of sun, music, medicine, and poetry

ARABIAN—today, a breed of horse descended from a strain

developed by desert Bedouins. Formerly the English called many

horses of Oriental blood Arabian, creating a great deal of confusion

to later historians of bloodlines. The so-called Arabians that helped

form the English Thoroughbred were frequently Turkish horses, of a strain bred to be diplomatic gifts. They were part Arabian.

ARES—Greek god of war

ASSURBANIPAL—King of Assyria, 669–626 B.C. A stone relief
shows him on a galloping horse, accurately shooting a bow while
seated on a saddle pad without girth or stirrups. Modern author J.
Spruytte has copied Assurbanipal's equipment and demonstrated
that it worked quite well (even before the invention of the recurved
bow).

ASSYRIA—an ancient empire centered in the upper valley of
the Tigris River, present-day Iraq; supplanted by the Persians.

ATHENA—Greek goddess of wisdom and the arts

ATHERTON, HUMPHREY—first Major General of the
Massachusetts Bay Colony

BERINGIA—the land-bridge that emerges between Alaska and
Siberia during glacial periods; currently it lies beneath the Bering
Strait

BILLABONG—In Australia, a streambed that fills with water only in
the rainy season

BUCEPHALUS—the horse tamed by twelve-year-old Alexander

the Great. He carried Alexander in battle until age thirty—a great

age for a horse—when he died of battle wounds in India.

BUZKAZHI—central Asian horseback game

CACIQUE—Spanish for chief, derived from an Arawak word

CÃONABO—a chief of the Arawak tribe, captured by

Columbus in 1494

CASPIAN HORSE—an ancient breed, rediscovered by American

Louise Firouz in 1965. Caspian horses are only forty inches high at

maturity, fast, gentle, and talented at jumping. They nearly became

extinct during the Iran–Iraq war, when they were driven before

advancing troops to clear the ground of land mines. Populations

now exist in Europe and America.

CAVALIER—a horseman. The word implies upper-class status

and military prowess. Capitalized, Cavalier means a supporter of

English King Charles I in his war with Parliament.

CHIVALRY—the medieval institution of knighthood, and the

ideals, code of conduct, and sanctioned privileges of knighthood

CIBOLA, SEVEN CITIES OF—legendary treasure cities of the

North American Southwest

CONQUISTADORES—Spanish conquerors of the Americas

CORONADO—a conquistador

COSSACKS—Russian cavalrymen or tribal fighters

DARIUS THE GREAT—King of Persia, 522–486 B.C. He is depicted

hunting lions from a chariot pulled by tiny horses. This was widely

assumed to be a case of artistic license, until similar tiny horses were

discovered by Louise Firouz (see Caspian horse).

DELHI SULTANATE—Islamic kingdom in northern India, 1206–1555

DEMETER—Greek goddess of agriculture, fertility, and marriage

DE SOTO, HERNANDO—Spanish discoverer of the Mississippi (1541)

DE VACA, ALVAR NÚÑEZ CABEZA—Spanish conquistador and mystic

DESTRIER—warhorse, charger

DIADIAPHOROS—three-toed South American precursor to thoatherium

EIGHT-UP—a team of eight horses to pull a wagon

EMPEROR MU'S HORSES—a strain of horse with great endurance,

called "Dragon Horses." They had small bony bumps on their foreheads resembling horns. Horns still occur in the Datong, an excellent Chinese endurance breed, and in the Moyle horse in North America. Mu Wang was the Zhou Dynasty ruler of China 1023–982 B.C.

EOCENE EPOCH—roughly 55 million years ago to 35 million years ago

EOHIPPUS—early ancestor of the horse

EPONA—Celtic goddess of horses and childbirth

ESTEBAN—African slave shipwrecked with de Vaca; he traveled among the American Indian tribes for eight years, learning to play medicine man. Later he led a preliminary expedition to discover the legendary treasure cities; he was captured and killed by the Zunis.

ETRUSCAN—pertaining to Etruria, a pre-Roman country of west-central Italy

FLY WHISK—a thick horsehair tassle used by a rider to swish flies off the horse

FOUNDATION SIRES AND DAMS—stallions and mares influential in the beginning of a breed

GALLEONS—large sailing ships of the 15th and 16th centuries

GENGHIS KHAN—Mongol conqueror of largest world empire, 1162–1227

HACK—a horse used for riding or driving

HIPPARIONS—an extinct family of three-toed horses that lived from the Miocene Epoch into the Pleistocene

HITTITES—an ancient people who formed an empire in Asia Minor and northern Syria about 2000–1200 B.C. Kikkulis the Mittanian, chariot master to Hittite king Sepululiumas, wrote the earliest horse-training manual yet discovered, about 1360 B.C. Modern horsemen, following his methods for a seven-month trial, found they produced an exceptionally fit animal.

HOBELAR—a light cavalryman of 13th and 14th centuries, mounted on a hobby horse

HOBBY HORSE—a fast breed of Irish horse, now extinct, a foundation breed for the English Thoroughbred

HORDE—a Mongol army

HOWDAH—a seat with canopy and railing, carried by an elephant

HUNS—a race of Asiatic nomads who overran Europe in the

4th and 5th centuries A.D., led by Attila

KAZAKHS—a formerly nomadic people of central Asia

KHAN—title given to rulers of the Mongols

LATERAL GAIT—any four-beat gait in which the horse moves

both legs on the same side of the body forward simultaneously.

Includes all forms of *paso*, *tølt*, amble, rack, rahvan, tripple, pace, etc.

The University of Zurich has established that the horse has fifty-five

possible gaits. Which are deemed "natural," "pure," and otherwise

desirable has been controversial at least since the time of the

18th-century French riding master La Gueriniere. The ambling

gaits have largely disappeared in Europe with the dominance

of Oriental breeding, but they remain in Asia, parts of Turkey,

the Americas, and South Africa.

LEVANT—the countries bordering the eastern Mediterranean

MACEDONIA—an ancient kingdom north of Greece

MANGALARGA MARCHADOR—a Brazilian breed of horse

MARCHA—Portuguese term for a lateral gait

MEDUSA—a mythological (Greek) woman with snakes for

hair and eyes that could turn mortals to stone. She was slain by
Perseus, and the winged horse Pegasus was born from a
drop of her blood.

MESOPOTAMIA—the ancient country between the Tigris and
Euphrates rivers

MIOCENE EPOCH—roughly 24 million years ago to 5 million years ago

MIOHIPPUS—three-toed horse of the Oligocene epoch

MOHAMMED—prophet and founder of Islam, 570–632 A.D.

OLIGOCENE EPOCH—roughly 34 million years ago to 25 million years ago

ORDER OF EQUITES—a Roman aristocratic order, copied from the
Greeks as a way to establish a cavalry. The first Equites were
given horses and privileges; later the privileges were sufficient
incentive to encourage horse breeding. This system formed the
basis of European chivalry; most noble European families trace
back to a soldier of fortune who received land in exchange for
riding for his king.

ORIENTAL HORSES—horse breeds originating in western or
central Asia

ORTA—the Mongolian postal service, stretching 5,000 miles. Unlike in the American Pony Express, one rider was expected to make the entire journey, sometimes up to 250 miles a day, changing horses along the way. The Pony Express lasted eighteen months, the *orta* seven centuries, until 1949.

PAD—an easy-gaited horse (Medieval term)

PANNIERS—a pair of baskets or packs carried by a pack animal

PASO—Spanish term for an ambling gait

PERCHERON—a draft horse breed originating in France

PERSIAN EMPIRE—an empire founded in the 6th century B.C. Based in what is modern Iran, it stretched from Egypt to modern Turkey, Greece to India. Conquered by Alexander the Great by 330 B.C.

POSEIDON—Greek god of the waters, earthquakes, and horses

PRZEWALSKI'S HORSE—a horse originating during the glacial period, running wild in Mongolia until the 1960s. Recently, zoo-bred Przewalski's Horses have been released on a reserve in Mongolia under protection of the government.

QUIVIRA—legendary treasure city

ROUNCY—a compact, sturdy horse, the mount of a knight's squire

SOLOMON—King of Israel in 10th century B.C., son of King David

SPANISH ARMADA—fleet sent by Spain to attack England in

    1588, defeated and destroyed by storms

STEPPE—a vast grassy plain, of southeastern Europe and Siberia

STONE AGE—earliest known period of human culture,

    characterized by use of stone tools

TENOCHTITLAN—ancient Aztec capital, on site of modern

    Mexico City. Hernan Cortés and his men rode into the city in

    apparent friendship in 1519. After the Spanish massacred a thousand

    unarmed dancers, general fighting broke out. Cortes retreated on

    June 30, 1520, the Noche Triste, losing eighty men and sixty horses.

    But Cortes soon returned and took the city by siege in August 1521.

THOATHERIUM—swift single-toed horse-analog of South America,

    which became extinct when the Americas rejoined. North American

    mammals outcompeted many of their South American counterparts.

THOROUGHBRED—the English racehorse breed developed by

crossing Oriental and native British breeds. The Thoroughbred is the world's fastest racehorse.

TRAVOIS—a primitive vehicle consisting of a platform or net supported by two long poles; the front ends are fastened to a horse or dog. In Russia it is called *drozkhy*, in Ireland a slide-car. The first form of vehicle drawn by animals, invented independently all over the world.

TURKMEN—variant of Turkoman, a formerly nomadic people of central Asia, or their horses

TUTANKHAMEN'S CHARIOTS—the most complete ancient chariots discovered, built for Egyptian king Tutankhamen in the 14th century B.C. They were light and strong, like modern racing sulkies.

YASSA—the system of law laid down by Genghis Khan. It contained explicit rules for handling horses. Riding them too hard or striking them was forbidden on pain of death.

ZEUS—Greek ruler of the heavens, father of the other gods.

Bibliography

"All books are about other books," author Betty Levin told me once. This book is about two books in particular: *Conquerors: The Roots of the New World Horsemanship*, by Deb Bennett, Ph.D., and *International Encyclopedia of Horse Breeds* by Bonnie Hendricks. Both are full of stories that span the sweep of time from the glacier age to the present. Both demolish myths and put in their place true stories that are even more fascinating.

Bennett, Deb, Ph.D. *Conquerors: The Roots of New World Horsemanship*. Solvang, Calif.: Amigo Publications, 1998.

Budiansky, Stephen. *The Nature of Horses: Exploring Equine Evolution, Intelligence, and Behavior*. New York: Simon & Schuster, Inc., 1997.

Clutton-Brock, Juliet. *Horse Power*. London: Natural History Museum Publications, 1992.

Cooke, Bill, ed. *Imperial China: The Art of the Horse in Chinese History*. Prospect, Ky.: Kentucky Horse Park & Harmony House Publishers, 2000.

Davis, Caroline, ed. *The Kingdom of the Horse*. New York: Howell Book House, 1998.

Dent, Anthony. *The Horse: Through Fifty Centuries of Civilization*. New York: Holt, Rhinehart and Winston, 1974.

Dent, Anthony, and Daphne Machin Goodall. *A History of British Native Ponies*. London: J. A. Allen, 1962.

Edwards, Elwyn Hartley. *The Encyclopedia of the Horse*. London: Dorling Kindersley, 1994.

Fox, Charles Philip. *A Pictorial History of Performing Horses*. New York: Bramhall House, 1960.

Hendricks, Bonnie L. *International Encyclopedia of Horse Breeds.* Norman, Okla., and London: University of Oklahoma Press, 1995.

Homer. *The Iliad.* Translated by Samuel Butler. Roslyn, N.Y.: Walter J. Black, Inc., 1942.

Hope, Lieutenant Colonel C. E. G., and G. N. Jackson, eds. *The Encyclopedia of the Horse.* New York: Viking Press, 1973.

Hyland, Ann. *The Warhorse 1250–1600.* Gloustershire, U.K.: Sutton Publishing, 1998.

Jankovich, Miklos. *They Rode into Europe.* New York: Charles Scribner's Sons, 1968.

Kimball, J. Davis. "Warrior Women of the Eurasian Steppes." *Archeology* 50: 1 (Jan./Feb., 1997): 44–51.

Mackay-Smith, Alexander. *Speed and the Thoroughbred.* Boston: The Derrydale Press, 2000.

Ripart, Jacqueline. *Horses of the World: From the Desert to the Racetrack.* New York: Harry N. Abrams, Inc., 2001.

Severin, Tim. *In Search of Genghis Khan.* New York: Atheneum, 1992.

Snader, Meredith L.,V.M.D. *Healing Your Horse: Alternative Therapies.* New York: Howell Book House, 1993.

Trippett, Frank, and the editors of Time-Life Books.
The First Horsemen. New York: Time-Life Books, 1974.

Vernam, Glenn R. *Man on Horseback*. New York: Harper and Row,
1964.